KT-488-119

How to use this book

This book has four stories for your child to read.

Get up! page 6
In the sun page 10
Mud page 14
Cat flap page 18

Before each story there are important activities which will help prepare your child for reading it. When he or she has read the story, there are further activities which will help reinforce what has been learnt.

- *Have fun talking about the pictures.*
- *Encourage your child to read the engaging stories again and again for fun and practice.*
- *Use the Star checklist on page 3 to build your child's confidence as he or she colours in a star after each activity.*

Six steps for reading success

1 *Practise reading the Speed sounds before each story.*
2 *Read the Green and Red words before each story.*
3 *Read the story.*
4 *Re-read the story to reinforce meaning.*
5 *Answer the questions about the story.*
6 *Practise reading the Speed words.*

Give your child lots of praise and encouragement. Have fun!

Story

I can read the Speed sounds.

I can read the Green words.

I can read the Red words.

I can read the story.

I can answer the questions about the story.

I can read the Speed words

Say the Speed sounds

Consonants

Ask your child to say the sounds (not the letter names) clearly and quickly, in and out of order. Make sure he or she does not add 'uh' to the end of the sounds, e.g. 'f' not 'fuh'.

f	l	m	n	r	s	v	z	sh	th	ng nk

b	c k ck	d	g	h	j	p	qu	t	w	x	y	ch

Each box contains one sound.

Vowels

Ask your child to say each vowel sound and then the word, e.g. 'a', 'at'.

at	hen	in	on	up

Story 1 Get up!

Read the Green words

For each word ask your child to read the separate sounds, e.g. 's-u-n' and then blend the sounds together to make the word, e.g. 'sun'. Sometimes one sound is represented by more than one letter, e.g. 'th', 'ou'. These are underlined.

get sun up ted Sam

bed of is

Read the Red words

Red words don't sound like they look. Read the words out to your child. Explain that he or she will have to stop and think about how to say the red words in the story.

<u>the</u> <u>out</u>

Story 1

Get up!

Introduction

This story is about a girl who has woken up on a sunny day.

The sun is up.

Get up! Get up!

Get up Sam.

Get up ted!

The sun is up.
Get out of bed.

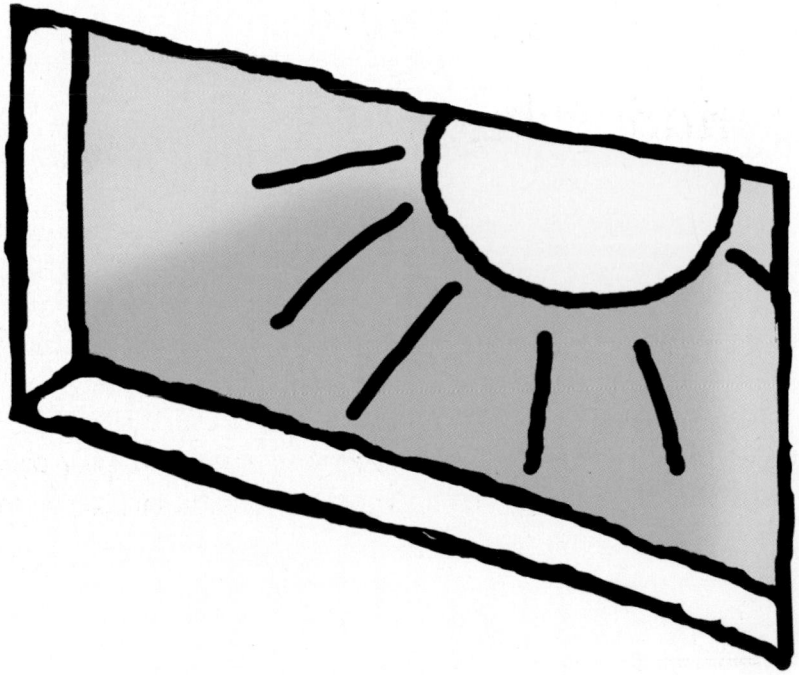

Ask your child:
Who does the girl want to get up?

Story 2 In the sun

Read the Green words

For each word ask your child to read the separate sounds, e.g. 'f-u-n' and then blend the sounds together to make the word, e.g. 'fun'. Sometimes one sound is represented by more than one letter, e.g. 'th'. These are underlined.

ran sun in jam fun a

sat had bun

Read the Red words

Red words don't sound like they look. Read the words out to your child. Explain that he or she will have to stop and think about how to say the red words in the story.

I the

Story 2

In the sun

Introduction

Do you like it when it's sunny? This is a story about a girl playing in the sun.

I ran in the sun.

I sat in the sun.

I had a jam bun in the sun.

I had fun in the sun.

Ask your child:

What three things did the girl do in the sun?

Story 3 Mud

Read the Green words

For each word ask your child to read the separate sounds, e.g. 'm-u-d', 'k-i-ck' and then blend the sounds together to make the word, e.g. 'mud', 'kick'. Sometimes one sound is represented by more than one letter, e.g. 'th', 'ck'. These are underlined.

mud kick in sit jump run

Read the Red words

Red words don't sound like they look. Read the words out to your child. Explain that he or she will have to stop and think about how to say the red words in the story.

I the

Story 3

Mud

Introduction

This is the story of a girl who likes messing around in mud!

I kick the mud.

I run in the mud.

I jump in the mud.

I sit in the mud.

Ask your child:
What do you think the girl likes doing most in the mud?

Story 4 Cat flap

Read the Green words

For each word ask your child to read the separate sounds, e.g. 'c-a-t' and then blend the sounds together to make the word, e.g. 'cat'. Sometimes one sound is represented by more than one letter, e.g. 'th'. These are underlined.

in cat sad fat rat a yum

big flap

Read the Red words

Red words don't sound like they look. Read the word out to your child. Explain that he or she will have to stop and think about how to say the red word in the story.

the

Story 4

Cat flap

Introduction

This story is about lots of different cats coming through cat flaps. Then, something else comes through . . .

In the cat flap

a fat cat . . .

In the cat flap

a sad cat . . .

In the cat flap

a big rat . . .

. . . yum yum!

Ask your child:
What do you think will happen to the rat?

Speed words for Story 1

Ask your child to read the words across the rows, down the columns and in and out of order, clearly and quickly.

up	is	the	get
sun	bed	ted	of

Speed words for Story 2

ran	sat	in	jam	fun
sun	the	had	bun	a

Speed words for Story 3

Ask your child to read the words across the rows, down the columns and in and out of order, clearly and quickly.

mud	kick	I	in
the	sit	jump	run

Speed words for Story 4

cat	yum	in	fat	the
sad	rat	big	a	flap

Help your child to read with phonics

Series created by
Ruth Miskin
Based on original stories by
Gill Munton and Ruth Miskin
Illustrated by
Tim Archbold

Published by
Oxford University Press
Great Clarendon Street
Oxford OX2 6DP

© Oxford University Press 2008

First published 2008
All rights reserved
This edition 2010

ISBN 9 780192 756138

10 9 8 7 6 5 4 3 2 1

Printed in China by Imago